Stories of *Hope* for Christian *Women*

Stories of
Hope
for Christian
Women

Based on True Experiences

VERONICA ALZAGA, LMFT

XULON PRESS

Xulon Press
2301 Lucien Way #415
Maitland, FL 32751
407.339.4217
www.xulonpress.com

Unless otherwise indicated, Scripture quotations taken from the
Holy Bible, New International Version (NIV). Copyright © 1973,
1978, 1984, 2011 by Biblica, Inc.™. Used by permission. All rights
reserved.

Printed in the United States of America.

ISBN-13: 978-1-6312-9354-2
Ebook: 978-1-6312-9355-9

Dedication

⌒

This book is dedicated to my husband, Ricardo, and my sons, Diego, Issac, and Abel, who inspire me to be the best version of myself. Love you guys more than words can ever say. With that said, it is a step of faith and obedience, as I know God has called me to write toward sharing knowledge and bringing hope to His people.

Table of Contents

Author's Note

Though I am a Licensed Marriage and Family Therapist, I have written this book outside my professional role. I am merely sharing the stories that have inspired and strengthened other women's walk in the faith, as well as my own Christian journey. With that said, this book is not intended to teach religion or spirituality. It is not about guiding or changing anyone's mind regarding their religious or spiritual practices. Instead, it is about encouraging and bringing hope to ladies who identify with the traditional Christian faith. For that matter, it is for anyone needing reassurance of God's active role in His children's lives.

While all the stories are based on true events, they have been purposefully modified for confidentiality reasons. Other than my name, all other names are fictitious, and any identifiable characteristics and details have been carefully changed. Nevertheless, the experiences are completely true in nature. However, any resemblance to anyone other than the main character of each narrative is entirely coincidental. Still, it is only expected that many may identify with any of the stories shared in this book and feel more encouraged and hopeful because of it, which is the main goal of this work.

Introduction

There are millions of women of faith worldwide, but each of their stories is so unique. Each Christian path is extraordinarily different from one another, as there are no two persons alike. Each woman is distinct from any other in regard to her life experiences, nonetheless, similar to many in her personal battles. There are a multitude of possible types of struggles. For some, the pains are obvious, such as a serious illness or the infidelity of a husband. In other instances, the hurt might be less palpable to observers or even to the sufferer, as in the case of spiritual doubt. Nevertheless, each is a significant life challenge in one way or another.

There are even those times when a situation may feel so unbearable that a woman might come to think that God has forgotten about her. In turn, she could fail to remember His incredible love and care for her. In those instances, some may even point to a lack of faith as the main issue, which may not be the case at all. Rather, there are circumstances that are so severe, even the strongest believer may feel weakened in faith. Even more, a life challenge coupled with any physical, emotional, or spiritual condition can certainly contribute to the inability to face tribulation. In those moments, more than ever, it is crucial to remember what God has promised during difficulties: "So do not fear, for I am with you; do not be dismayed, for I am your God. I will strengthen you and help you; I will uphold you with my righteous right hand" (Isa. 41:10).

It is clear then that God cares for His children and that He is at the center of all help. There is also no doubt that He has the power to change situations. However, God works in mysterious ways and appears many times more focused on spiritual growth than solving individual problems. For example, while He does not need humans' help, He has called on His people to help one another "Carry each other's burdens and this way you will fulfill the law of Christ" (Gal. 6:2). Additionally, of great importance, He has also directed His people to love one another. "My command is this: Love each other as I have loved you" (John 15:12).

Among the many ways to show support and care during others' time of need, encouraging and sharing hope is definitely a great act of love. In particular, for women, who tend to be more socially driven than men, sharing and hearing from others is essential to their overall wellbeing, but crucial during the more difficult times. For such reason, this book aims to encourage and share hope through what God has done for other ladies. During this process, each woman may be reminded that regardless of her individual situation,

God's character does not change because of what she is facing. On the contrary, the loving Father, Jesus, and the Holy Spirit continue to always be there to love, rescue, comfort, guide, and support.

Ask:
Irene Learned That God Could Do It All

⌒

Ask and it will be given to you; seek and you will
find; knock and the door will be open to you.

Matthew 7:7

*I*rene and Victor were young newlyweds, and as expected,
they had their hearts full of hopes and dreams for their
future. But more than how much they loved each other, they
had chosen to share their lives because they genuinely believed
they had what it took to make a marriage work. They both had
come from dysfunctional households where the fathers had
abandoned the families. For such reason, they were determined to make their little nest a lasting and loving home. In

addition to sharing their desire to stay married for life, they also agreed on many important areas, as they shared their ethnicity and had comparable values. However, their religious affiliations were not the same. While they had both been raised Catholic, Irene had been studying with the Jehovah's Witnesses for two years prior to dating Victor. Yet, she had not taken the last step to be baptized, as there were still some questions and she was not sure that faith was for her.

Although Irene and Victor respected each other's religious beliefs, they both agreed that raising a family under two spiritual views might be too challenging and confusing for all the children they planned on having. Unable to compromise about what religion to follow, they began praying for God's guidance on whether the family should practice Catholicism or become Jehovah's Witnesses. As time went by, they opted for finding a new religion that incorporated what they both liked from their existing spiritual practices. And after a bit of research and to their surprise, they began to attend a church of another Christian denomination.

Irene connected immediately with the new Christian teachings, but Victor was not as convinced and continuously challenged many of the new concepts. Additionally, he found giving up certain aspects of his lifestyle was extremely difficult. In particular, his heavy drinking and enjoyment of pornography and gruesome movies were all things Irene did not agree with. That is when they began to have strong arguments. Irene even thought she had made a big mistake by marrying Victor. But with a baby on the way already, she did not say anything to anyone about what she was going through in her marriage and focused instead on growing spiritually.

Irene began to pray and read her Bible every day. The more she would read, the stronger her faith would become. Then one evening, her Satan-worshipping next-door neighbors began to fight loudly, as they usually did. Irene was suspicious that they would even get physical with each other because of the loud sounds she heard. Out of ideas, Irene took out her Bible and began to read out loud, as she paced from one end of her apartment to the other. Immediately, her neighbors became completely quiet. She first worried that maybe something terrible had occurred next door, as there seemed to be no logical explanation for the sudden and complete silence, but then she thought it had been the power of God's word. After that experience, she began praying, reading the Bible out loud, and playing worship songs all the time. She was still not sure how it worked, but she was certain there was power in the Bible and prayer.

As time went by, Irene became tired of the neighbors' constant fights and also wondered if her marriage would improve if they moved out of the apartment, where Victor had lived alone before marrying her. She also did not want her children to grow up in such environment, but her husband did not see it the same way. On the contrary, Victor did not want to move, as he thought it would be impossible to find another apartment at that price. Yet, Irene was certain God would open a way for them to move, if she just prayed with faith. She began to do that right after Victor denied her request to move.

Not too long after Irene began to pray for that need, Victor came home and shared that he had been offered work in another city. Without even hearing all the details of the job, she excitedly suggested he take the offer. He did, but he still did not agree to move. Actually, things became even worse for the family, as he had little time left for them due to all the time spent commuting to his new job. By then, Irene learned that God sometimes does things in steps over a period of time, so she did not become discouraged. Quite the opposite, she prayed even more fervently for a place to move to.

Then one evening, Victor came home and told Irene he was shocked, but his employer was offering to rent him a larger apartment for the same amount they were paying now. Even more, he said the rent included all the utilities. While Victor was happy about the apartment, he was confused, as it was a residence reserved for employees who had been working much longer than him. On the other hand, Irene was not surprised at all and happily began to pack.

She then prayed for her and her husband to get baptized in the Christian faith, which they did. She also prayed with great faith for her husband's heavy drinking, pornography use, and attraction to scary and gruesome movies to decrease, which then stopped. She even proudly shared multiple times that one of her Christian triumphs was when her husband told her she could throw away his collection of horror movies. Instead of just getting rid of them, she took a hammer and destroyed them piece by piece to make sure no one else could ever watch what she believed did not honor God. Since then,

Irene continued praying with faith and believing that God can do it all.

Hope in Action

God has the power to answer, provide, and open a way where there seems to be none.

Write about the most recent time when God answered, provided, or opened a way where there seemed like there was no possibility. Then thank Him for it.

_____

_____

_____

_____

Write about a situation that you may be experiencing that requires of God's answer, provision, or power to open a way. Then pray about it.

_____

_____

_____

_____

_____

Believe:
Esther Discovered the Power in the Name of Jesus

~~

Do not let your hearts be troubled. Trust in
God; trust also in me.

John 14:1

*E*sther was a married woman in her thirties. She loved her
husband and children with all her heart. She was determined to be a good wife and wonderful mother, but at times it
was difficult, as her fears, anxiety, and depression would get in
the way. Also, early on in her life, she had learned that letting
her emotions be seen was a sign of weakness; therefore, she
wouldn't dare tell anyone about her personal struggles. On
the contrary, she would pretend she was happy and she lived

the kind of life she had always dreamed with her husband, which was not the case. Her only refuge was God, to whom she would cry out and pray for strength. It was not that there wasn't anyone in her life who wanted to support her, rather, she was too afraid to accept the help.

In particular, one of her sisters would often invite her to her church and to women's Christian retreats. But Esther was fearful about so many things that she could not bear the thought of having to leave her children with someone else. Also, risking putting herself in an unfamiliar atmosphere was completely out of the question. For her, the more control she could have over her environment, the safer she thought her children, husband, and she would be.

Then one day, after much insistence from her sister and without really understanding why, Esther accepted an invitation to attend a women's weekend retreat at the church Houses of Light in Northridge, California. However, as the date of the event got closer, she wanted to change her mind about going, but feared having to explain the real reason for backing out of the invitation. There was also, deep down in her heart, a tiny glimpse of hope that maybe she could learn something that would improve her emotional situation. She wondered how her life could change if she felt less depressed and anxious.

Her sadness and fearfulness were rooted in all the trauma she had experienced growing up. Her father had abandoned her completely, her mother had been emotionally and phys-ically abusive, people had tried to kidnap her multiple times, and she had endured sexual abuse from both family members and strangers since her earliest memories. To Esther, the world was a scary place, where terrible things occurred unexpectedly.

When the weekend of the retreat came, Esther was sure she had made a big mistake, as her anxiety had reached an unbearable level, but she could not find the courage to cancel. Pushing herself more than she thought was possible, she mustered the strength to attend the women's gathering. On the Friday she arrived at the event, she was experiencing sensory overload due to being surrounded by so many people, rules and schedules to follow, and being out of her familiar environment. However, sleeping out of her bedroom was probably the hardest things for her, as she had to share a large cabin with many other ladies, which meant she had no control over anything.

On Saturday morning, she was desperate to go back home, but there seemed no way to escape her situation, as she was on a mountain with no phone reception. By Saturday afternoon though, something caught Esther's attention, after hearing one of the presenters talked about freedom in Christ. She wasn't sure she understood all the presentation, but the idea that Jesus could heal anything was new to her. Additionally, she was invited by the church leaders to make a list of the people and circumstances in her life that had caused her pain and to give it to Jesus. Esther was not quick to agree and felt so confused by what she was hearing. She just could not understand how naming those who had hurt her could possibly change anything for her.

As the weekend continued, she made the decision to put to the test what she was being told. Esther took a piece of paper and wrote down all the names of the people who had harmed her throughout her life and even included the physical characteristics of the strangers who had sexually abused her, since she didn't know their names. After that, she was guided to forgive all those people. That was when it really became hard for Esther, as it made no sense to give forgiveness to those who did not deserve it. No one on her list was asking her to forgive them or had ever seemed sorry for what they had put her through. But as difficult as it was for her to do, she verbalized the words of forgiveness, thinking she had nothing to lose. Additionally, she was very curious about what could happen if what she was being told was true. What if forgiving was actually freeing her from any tie to those who had caused her so much pain?

Then during the last event on Sunday, Esther literally felt a huge weight lifted off her. It was as if she had been carrying around a tremendous heavy rock, and suddenly someone had removed it from her back. She felt so light and liberated, there was a moment she felt as if she could almost fly. For at least one hour, Esther danced around and sang hymns of worship and gratitude. It was not until she noticed a familiar face staring at her that she realized what she had been doing, but she was so perfectly happy, nothing at all seemed to worry her.

That day, Esther's life began to change, and with time, her anxiety, depression, and all her fears improved so much she was able to enjoy her life for the very first time. What's more, she began to share the gift she received with other ladies by supporting them to attend that same retreat. But more than anything else, she shared her story and encouraged everyone around her to believe in Christ, His love, and the power in His name.

Hope in Action

Believe that God has the power to heal all.

Write about a time when God healed an area of your life. Then thank Him for it.

_____

_____

_____

_____

_____

Write about a need(s) troubling your heart and pray about it in the name of Jesus.

_____

_____

_____

_____

_____

Call:
Karen Called on God for Help

Call to me and I will answer you and tell you
great and unsearchable things you do not know.

Jeremiah 33:3

Karen grew up in a very dysfunctional environment. Her
father abandoned the home when her mother was pregnant with her. As she grew up, she saw her father just a handful
of times, but every time she would end up feeling disheartened
due to his lying and lack of paternal responsibility. On the other
hand, Karen's mother did her best to provide and care for her
and her siblings, but it was far from perfect. The stressors of
life and lack of support and knowledge would often get in the
way of her mother's good intentions. As a result, Karen was

forced to co-parent and deal with her mom's constant mood swings and unfair demands.

Karen's upbringing, repetitive changes in paternal figures, and history of abuse ultimately led her to having a distorted concept of what a healthy family could look like. She would often wonder why life had to be so incredibly harsh. But as she began learning new things at the university she attended, a desire to have a different type of family was born. Among other things, she dreamed of becoming a loving, kind, and understanding mother.

Unfortunately, Karen had not yet developed the skills to have the kind of home she wanted when she had her first daughter and then a second child. Her husband had also grown up in a very difficult household and lacked the know-how to guide and support her and their children. In addition, he also struggled with bad habits from his single years, which brought about further issues to his role as a husband and parent. In short, Karen's family didn't look the way she had dreamed, and time was not stopping to give her a break. Before she realized it, her oldest child was in middle school and began exhibiting odd behaviors, such as isolating, having anger outbursts, withdrawing, not wanting to be touched, having poor grades, and a negative attitude. Karen loved her daughter very much but didn't understand what was happening to her. She would often try to talk to her teen, but her daughter wouldn't open up. Instead, she would become verbally aggressive and withdraw from the family. Karen wasn't sure what to think and attributed her daughter's issues to dealing with the physical and emotional changes of puberty.

Karen was a woman who genuinely believed in the power of prayer and regularly spent much time praying for her family, and specially for her oldest daughter. Then one day, she felt led to ask her daughter again about how she was feeling and was shocked with the response. Her teenager shared that she was being bullied at school and hated her life. She was glad her daughter had opened up to her, but felt inadequate to help her, as Karen had lived a similar situation during her school years and had overcome it by ignoring it.

Her first reaction was to run to God and pray for guidance on what to do. A few days later, Karen was waiting at a medical office when she overheard another patient talking about homeschooling. After the other patient left, Karen shyly asked the receptionist about it. And without even knowing where or how she would do it; Karen came home that day and told her oldest daughter she did not have to go back to public school, she was going to homeschool her. She was hoping her daughter would be thrilled with the news, but the girl's answer alarmed her. She told Karen she felt relieved more than anything, as she had been feeling so overwhelmed and misunderstood that she had already made the decision to take her life in the near future. Karen was first speechless, but after pulling herself together, she told her daughter she loved her very much and they would figure it out together.

Over time, Karen's oldest daughter received psychotherapy, made new friends, and began the journey of emotional recovery. Her relationship with the family and her school performance also improved significantly, which in turn made a tremendous difference in other areas of the teen's life. As for Karen, she can truly say that God answered her call for help with her daughter and to become the type of mother she dreamed of.

Hope in Action

Call on the one who has the power to change circumstances and give you what you need.

Write about a time when God answered a prayer in a way you did not expect. Then thank Him for it.

_____

_____

_____

_____

_____

Write about a need(s) you are asking God to help you with and pray about it.

_____

_____

_____

_____

_____

Courage:
Julia Went to God for Courage

Be strong and courageous. Do not be afraid or terrified because of them, for the LORD your God goes with you; he will never leave you nor forsake you.

Deuteronomy 31:6

Julia had been told early on in her life that she would not be able to become a mother due to an abnormality with her uterus. She was still young when she first heard the news, and even found it a relief. She was not too sure she wanted to deal with crying babies and the challenges of motherhood, but all that changed after she fell in love. More than anything, she wanted to have a child with Carlos, the man she dreamed of growing old with.

When they were finally able to conceive a baby, it was one of the happiest days of their lives. In particular, Julia was glowing and began wearing maternity clothing before anyone could even tell she was pregnant. She wanted so much to share her baby news with the world. On his end, Carlos made sure she ate well, she didn't carry anything heavy, and almost treated her as a baby herself. They both wanted a son and that was what the ultrasound indicated. They were told they would be having a healthy and strong baby boy. They were ecstatic to hear the news and could hardly wait to hold their son. As the months passed, Julia's abdomen continued to grow. Carlos spent much time hugging her stomach and talking to the baby. They had even picked the name for their child, who was to be the fourth Carlos, as it was a tradition in his family that the first son would have the father's name. Everything was going as planned with the pregnancy and it seemed they couldn't be happier as a couple.

Then the last thing Julia ever imagined occurred. She found out Carlos was with another woman. In a split second, all her dreams seemed to crumble before her eyes. She wished that it was just a nightmare, but Carlos admitted to his actions. Overnight, their fairytale love story disappeared. Julia decided she would not raise her baby under the care of a man she could not trust and asked Carlos that they go their separate ways. Julia was broken hearted and couldn't see a way their relationship could work if she could not trust him. Although she asked him to leave their home, she agreed that for the best interest of her son, she would allow him to be present at the delivery. As for a relationship with her, she was so hurt she wanted nothing to do with him. However, she also didn't want to live alone towards the end of her pregnancy.

Around the time Julia and Carlos separated, her brother was going through a difficult personal time and needed a place to live. Her brother moved in and everything seemed fine. Julia was so happy to help her sibling and also to have someone keep her company until the baby was born. Her brother spent much time out of the home and whenever she would ask, he would always say he was looking for a job or something similar. Then one evening, as she was getting ready to make dinner, she noticed something strange. A couple of young males seemed to be snooping around the back door of her small apartment patio door. When she asked through the window if they were looking for someone, they said they played soccer with her brother and wanted to talk to him. Her brother came out to talk to them while she continued cooking in her kitchen.

Then suddenly, she heard a desperate shout outside: "Julia, they are going to kill me!" She loved her brother very much, and without even thinking about her baby or herself, she grabbed a long knife and hid it under her arm. She ran out to find her brother bleeding from the head as he was being dragged off the property. She asked one of the males what was going on, but he just ignored her. She knew she could have stabbed at least one of the two men, but thought it would make things worse for all. Instead, she looked at the license plates of the car they were driving away and ran back into her apartment to call the police. After giving the police all the information, she began to pray as never before that God would take control of everything and save her brother's life. A few minutes later, which felt like an eternity to her, a police operator called her back, saying they had her brother and he was being transported to a nearby hospital.

Julia and her family were so grateful God spared her brother's life and gave him a second chance. And to everyone's surprise, he had no more than minor injuries. He confessed to the family that he had gotten himself in trouble with drug-related issues, but something incredible had occurred. He said just as those men were driving away with him to go kill him in Mexico, their car had stopped without any apparent reason. It was then the police found them. The family could hardly believe how God had saved him and how courageously Julia had behaved. She was certain God gave her the courage and guidance. As for her baby, she delivered a beautiful healthy son. And yes, the baby's father was present at the delivery.

Hope in Action

Great courage comes from God!

Write about a time when God gave you the courage to do something you were not sure you could do. Then thank Him for it.

_____

_____

_____

_____

_____

Write about a situation(s) you may be facing that requires a great deal of courage. Then pray about it.

_____

_____

_____

_____

_____

Deliverance:
Paula Was Delivered from Harm

⌒

The LORD is my rock, my fortress and my deliverer; my God is my rock, in whom I take refuge. He is my shield and the horn of my salvation, my stronghold.

Psalm 18:2

Paula was twenty-four years old when her mother mentioned she was having some medical concerns. Her mom asked if she would accompany her to the doctor, as she was thinking she had begun the process of menopause. Paula thought nothing of it, as her mama was in her forties and it made sense in her family.

On the day of the medical visit, everything seemed to go as normal, except Paula was asked to stay for a short meeting with the doctor following the checkup. She sensed something was terribly wrong as her mother seemed pale and was acting extremely nervous. With a startled voice, Paula's mother told her she was pregnant and was not sure what she would do. The doctor went on to discuss the possible risks to the baby and offered to conduct testing for Down Syndrome.

Paula, concerned for the wellbeing of her mother but also a strong anti-abortion believer, asked about the risks the test could pose to the unborn. After hearing there was a possibility of harming the baby in the test procedure, Paula recommended against it. She then turned to her mother, and in front of the doctor asked in a firm voice if she was considering an abortion. Paula felt relieved after hearing her respond that she would keep her baby no matter what. The next step was figuring out how to tell her mother's husband, who was much older than her.

After assisting in giving the father-to-be the news of the baby, Paula made the decision to support her mother through the pregnancy. She put her college studies on hold and began accompanying her mom to her job, as at times her mother's work required heavy lifting and pushing. When it came time for the ultrasound, everyone was excited and grateful to hear that there was a healthy baby girl on the way. In particular, Paula felt so satisfied with herself, as she had been praying vehemently and was making great efforts to support the pregnancy.

Then one evening, as Paula was sitting in the family's living room watching television, she heard a loud knocking at the front door. There was a male voice claiming to be a police

officer. As expected, she rushed and opened the door. After
seeing the two men standing there were not in uniforms, she
quickly tried to close it, but it was too late. One of the males
had put in his foot to hold the door open. After forcing their
way into the house, one of them put a gun to Paula's head. She
immediately thought of her pregnant mother, who was resting
in the back bedroom and what it could mean to the pregnancy,
but Paula had faith.

Paula was not sure how God would do it, but she knew
He had always delivered her from less challenging situations.
Two men with a gun were sure not going to stop Him. With a
firmness in her hand, she gently moved the gun away from her
head and confidently asked the men to state their business.
The younger man told her that his uncle had been very hurt
during a recent assault in the neighborhood, where a significant amount of money had been taken. He insisted that it had
been a teenage boy who lived in her home. The only young
male was her only brother. She sure did not think it was him,
but those men seemed pretty certain that was the case. After
planting the seed of the idea that there was no way her little
brother had done it, as he had been at a high school dance the
day they said the theft had occurred, she offered to let them
search the home.

Although she knew very well her brother was sleeping
upstairs, she proposed to call her stepfather to assist them
in looking around. She even told the younger man she also
loved her family and could only imagine his anger. She then
asked him for his contact number and promised to call him if

she heard anything about the robbery. The older man, who appeared to be the bodyguard, insisted she was lying, but the younger male told her he wished he had met her under different circumstances. He even gave her a phone number, which turned out to be fake.

After the two men left, Paula began shaking and told the rest of the family what had happened. Her brother said they were probably looking for the neighbor across the street who also lived in a similar home. Even the police couldn't believe she had been so calm during such an occurrence and that the two men had not hurt anyone. As for Paula, she was sure God had delivered her and her family from such a dangerous situation.

Hope in Action

Do you believe God can deliver you from any situation no matter how small or big?

Write about a time when God delivered you from a difficult situation. Then give Him thanks.

_____

_____

_____

_____

_____

Write about a difficult situation that requires from God deliverance. Then pray about it.

_____

_____

_____

_____

_____

A gift for you

Praying you are feeling better and have
a speedy recovery! Love Donna Burns xo
From Donna Burns

amazon Gift Receipt

Send a Thank You Note

You can learn more about your gift or start a return here too.

Scan using the Amazon app or visit
https://a.co/d/6mnfMNi

Stories of Hope for Christian Women: Based on True Experiences
Order ID: 114-2572331-4577054   Ordered on October 23, 2021

Depend:
Andrea Received Money
from Heaven

⌐⌐

For I am the LORD, your God, who takes hold
of your right hand and says to you, do not fear;
I will help you.

Isaiah 41:13

ndrea and her husband, Tony, had both grown up in sin-
gle-parent homes. They were both very proud of their
mothers and grateful to them for working so hard to be the
best providers they each could. However, they both understood that not having a mother at home had led to them to
being cared by extended family, friends, and babysitters, which
had not always been the best situation. For this reason, when

Andrea and Tony got married, they decided she would not seek employment, so she could focus on taking care of their children until they were school age. That meant they would have to live with one income for many years, which they knew was going to be very challenging. Because they really believed that the healthiest environment for their children would be a parent staying home to guide and watch over them, they agreed to make any necessary sacrifices.

Andrea's husband was a hardworking man, but his income was not always sufficient to meet their financial responsibilities. And even with her creative ideas to stretch his paycheck and save everywhere she could, there were times when the money was just not enough for their needs. On those days, she would try to figure things out by herself to avoid adding additional stress to her husband's already heavy load. Instead, she would go to God and pray for more wisdom to manage the finances and for provision for their needs. She would also pray often that she would never forget it was God on whom they depended for everything.

There was a particular month when Andrea felt more frustrated about their money situation. She had tried all she could think of, but she only had so much money left to spend. In faith, she had written a check to pay for one of their utility bills, but she knew there was simply not enough money in the bank. She also needed to buy food to last until her husband's next payday, but was not sure how she could do it. She really tried that day to be at peace, trusting that God would provide, as He had done some other times, but she couldn't see how that could be possible. All she could think of was to borrow money from her family, but she didn't want to be a burden, worry them, or make her husband seem as if he was not a good enough provider. Out of ideas, she decided that she was not going to be able to do both, pay her bill and buy groceries, so of course, she chose food for her children.

While she was driving to the supermarket, she went in prayer to God and asked for His help one more time. She sure had no idea how He could do it, but she understood that just because she could not solve her own problem, that did not mean He could not either. Then something strange happened. As she was driving through a parking lot, a strong wind lifted leaves that had fallen from a nearby tree, a common occurrence in the fall. What surprised her was that with those dried up leaves, there seemed to be dollar bills flying around. She first thought they had to be fake, but as they continued to fly around her car, she stopped her vehicle. Then she feared it could be one of those television games, where they trick you, but she didn't care if she had to make a fool of herself, as she desperately needed the money. She got out of her car and began to jump and run around to catch the flying money. It was not a lot of cash, but it was enough to buy more food for her children.

While the money she found did not solve her money problem, she felt so happy to be able to buy a little more food. Then as she was standing in line at the supermarket to pay for the food she was buying, there in front of her in the ground was a $20 bill. She politely asked the elderly woman in front of her if she had dropped it, but the lady said it was not hers. She also asked the cashier about it, but was told to keep it, as the money could not be put into the money drawer. At that moment, Andrea started realizing God was helping her. She quickly paid for what she was buying and went straight to the bank. To her even greater surprise, there was yet another $20 bill on floor next to the teller machine. She was certain then that God had answered her prayers. With tears of joy and a heart full of gratitude, she thanked God for sending her exactly the money she needed to cover the check and buy sufficient food for her children, until her husband's next paycheck. More than anything, Andrea was grateful to depend on God for everything.

Hope in Action

To depend on God brings great peace.

Write about a time when you depended on God to take care of a situation. Then thank Him for it.

_____

_____

_____

_____

_____

Write about a situation(s) where you need to depend on God's help, but have not, then pray about it.

_____

_____

_____

_____

_____

Faith: Victoria Waited on God for a Husband

Now faith is being sure of what we hope for and certain of what we do not see.

Hebrew 11:1

Even the sound of her sweetheart's voice would make Victoria's heartbeat faster. She would spend her days daydreaming of the last moment with him, as she tried to contain her desire to see him again. It was so obvious that she was completely in love with him. But how could she not be so enamored or at least think she was, at sixteen years of age? Maybe there was some truth to the saying that love was blind, as Victoria could see no wrong in her boyfriend. Even when others would point out his abnormal behavior, it was so easy for her dismiss and find excuses for him; she would say he was busy, he was distracted, he was poor, or he simply did not have to follow traditional dating customs. It was as if she had created a list of prepared responses to explain to others or herself his unusual behavior, which she either didn't see or didn't want to believe was true.

The girl in her had fallen in love for the first time, while desperately trying to hold on to something to endure her difficult home environment. Victoria was growing up in a dysfunctional family and she had finally found someone who would tell her she was beautiful, wonderful, and unconditionally loved, which appeared to be the opposite message she was receiving at home. Her boyfriend was someone to turn to for attention and for physical and emotional affection. Unfortunately, he also had a dark secret, which he had not shared or Victoria did not want to hear.

Either way, eight years of a roller coaster relationship went by until she could no longer handle her life at home. For fear of losing the only thing that made her happy, she went against her traditional values and moved out to live with him.

The first six months of living with her boyfriend felt like the happiest of her life, until that cold afternoon. She came back from work to a dark house and a letter from her beloved sitting on the kitchen table. As she began to read, she quickly realized it was his confession. In shock, she felt as if her heart had stopped beating and she struggled to breathe or think. In an instant, all of her dreams had crumbled. Then, as if in a movie, she saw her life with him run through her mind, but it was not a happy ending. She truly was in total disbelief, as she read that he was married in another country and had a second child recently born.

Learning about his deception would have scared off any woman, but not a codependent one who took him back after his pleading, crying, and saying she was the true love of his life. One year later, she was pregnant by him, and again felt she was the happiest woman on the planet. She was certain their child would bring them closer together and could hardly wait to meet her little one.

Victoria never imagined that looking into her baby's eyes would change the course of her life. As she finally held her newborn in her arms for the very first time, she felt an unimaginable love and desire to protect her child. In that same moment, she made a promise to herself and her son that she would not let her boyfriend hurt him and put him through the same emotional journey she had experienced. Shortly after the baby's birth and with her heart in pieces, she left that man, began working on her faith, and devoted herself to her boy, work, college, and praying. As her faith increased, she began to heal from the breakup and even began to think she could find love again.

Victoria made a list of ten traits she would want in a good husband, and spent the next two years praying about it every day. Then one day, an old friend invited her to a double date with her cousin Daniel. From what she remembered of her friend's relative, Victoria was not interested. In an effort to get out of the invitation, she told her friend that if her cousin really wanted to take her out on a date, he could call her himself. To her great surprise, not too long after that, Victoria was having coffee with her friend's cousin, Daniel. What's more, she figured that if she had agreed to meet him, she might as well see how many of the ten husband must-have items on the list he met. She was surprised to find out that he met all ten of the qualities she was looking for in a husband.

What was more amazing, it seemed he was doing the same thing to her. He even discussed marriage, which someone else might have thought was irrational on the first date, but not a woman of faith who was waiting for God's answer on who to marry. Daniel was funny, intelligent, and had a beautiful heart. Victoria was so certain it was God's doing, she even returned home that evening and told her mother He had showed her the man she would marry, but her mother didn't share her excitement. On the other hand, Victoria changed her prayers from request to gratitude, as she was sure God had answered her husband prayer in His perfect time.

Victoria was probably right, as she has been married to Daniel for almost twenty years.

Hope in Action

Remember that God answers His people's prayers with yes, no, or later.

Write about a time when you had faith God would answer a prayer and He did, even if the answer was no or later. Then thank Him for it.

_____

_____

_____

_____

_____

Write about a situation(s) where you need to have more faith that God will answer, even if His answer is no or later. Then pray about it.

_____

_____

_____

_____

_____

Guidance: Veronica Followed God's Direction

Whether you turn to the right or to the left,
your ears will hear a voice behind you, saying
"This is the way; walk in it."

Isaiah 30:21

Veronica was a Mexican, middle-aged woman who lived with her husband and children in California. She was a devoted Christian and enjoyed helping at North County Church of Christ. She had served in different church ministries, from teaching Sunday school to serving in the counseling area. But it had been some time since she had been involved in a specific ministry, as she had become so busy as a mother, wife, and with work, there was no time left for anything else. Specifically, her work as a counselor at a mental health clinic was demanding and constantly left her feeling drained without any energy to do more. She had also opened up her counseling private practice, which was definitely a new endeavor and kept her even busier. As much as she believed in serving God's people, she just could not see how.

Veronica hoped that one day, God would open up a way and guide her on when and where to serve the church again, but she was definitely not expecting to have to leave the country to do it. To her great surprise, she received a call from Great Cities Missions in Texas, inviting her to be part of a missionary trip to Guatemala. As humbled as she felt to receive the invitation, she immediately thought it would be difficult for her to attend, due to all her responsibilities and the cost involved. Yet she was not quick to say no, and instead responded that she would pray about it and talk to her husband and her church before deciding.

On that same day, she discussed the invitation with her husband. As she thought he would, he reminded her they were on a tight budget. As much as she wanted to go on the missionary trip, she knew her husband was correct, and she was not about to go against his decision. Nevertheless, she told him she would pray about it, which he thought was a reasonable approach to the situation. That same night, she began to pray and asked that God would guide them and make it obvious if He wanted her to go.

The next day, she talked to the benevolence team at her church. To her great surprise, within one week she was informed that they would contribute financially to cover most of her trip. Wow! She could hardly believe it! Veronica was so excited that she immediately shared her good news with a close Christian woman, who said she would provide the rest of the money needed to make the trip. Veronica was sure then that God was guiding her to go serve His people.

What a humbling experience it was for Veronica to travel to another country to serve. She was able to counsel missionary ladies who had gathered in Guatemala from many Spanish-speaking countries. Never in her dreams had she imagined God would use her to bless others in that capacity. She also grew spiritually in the process. Her faith became stronger and she was so inspired by other's stories of sacrifice and love for God's ministry. She was able to see how many women with little resources and numerous responsibilities were serving God's people around the world.

Hope in Action

From the simples to the most important decisions, God can guide and help.

Write about a time where God guided an important decision in your life. Then thank Him for it.

_____

_____

_____

_____

_____

Write about a situation(s) where you need to ask for God's guidance. Then pray about it.

_____

_____

_____

_____

_____

Help:
Emily Cried Out to God

The righteous cry out, and the LORD hears them; he delivers them from all their troubles.

Psalms 34:17

*E*mily was a woman devoted to God's word. Though she was fairly new to the Christian faith, she prayed daily, read her Bible, and was committed to honoring God in all the areas of her life. What a beautiful thing! She was truly experiencing her first love for Christ. Her husband Benjamin, on the other hand, was not as enthusiastic as she was. There were times he would even become frustrated with her, as she would take any opportunity to share Christ's teachings with him and their young children. It almost seemed that the more she learned about the Bible, the more they were growing apart in their faith. However, one thing they both agreed on was that spirituality was individual, and each person had the free will to choose what was best for him or her.

On his end, Benjamin was also struggling with the new expectations for his role as a spiritual leader, spouse, and father. Moreover, he had been raised under a different religion and could not understand Emily's insistence that they attend church weekly and that he give up his worldly lifestyle. Additionally, he was a very intelligent and technical man, which he said made it harder for him to simply accept the idea of a Creator, Savior, and the Holy Spirit. Nevertheless, he would respect Emily's beliefs about the Bible and would even entertain her thoughts at times. Then, an unforeseen situation occurred, which shook his entire believe system about God and even made Emily question her new faith.

On a cool winter evening, their family received a call that no one should ever get. They were informed that his brother had instantly passed away in a terrible vehicle accident. To say the least, she was horrified, and he was in shock. Without talking much over the next few days, they went through the funeral procedures. As time went by, Emily continued to be as supportive as possible, but Benjamin shut down and distanced himself from the family. He would hardly sleep and spent long hours in his office researching. It was as if he was on a mission to find the answers for the sudden death of his brother. In such process, he began to study various religions and spiritual practices. Without meaning to or even knowing it, he had created a routine that did not include his wife or children. On the contrary, he would isolate himself for longer periods of time, and when he did spend time with her, he would share why he doubted of the existence of a Creator, as she knew it. Specifically, why he was not sure Jesus was the only way.

Emily prayed more than ever, tried to stand firm in Christ, and asked her husband not to discuss his doubts in front of their children. And while he abstained from talking to his children about his spiritual struggles, he would not stop sharing information about other religions and his many questions with Emily. It reached a point where she began to wonder and question her spiritual beliefs. She truly felt confused in her faith and desperately cried out to God for help. She wanted a sign from God or anything that would confirm that what she believed was true and that she would not get lost in her faith because of what her husband was experiencing.

Shortly after that prayer, she was having tea by herself early one morning, after her husband had left to go to work. Then her oldest son, Ben, who was no more than nine years old, went directly to find her in the kitchen, after he woke up. Ben seemed a little surprised about a dream he had the previous night. He shared that even though he was certain he had not left his home, he had a dream that was so real and vivid it felt as if he had gone somewhere. At first, Emily thought Ben was just being a child with an active imagination. But as he began to relate his dream, she ran for paper and pen and began to write it all down. With every detail Ben shared, Emily could feel a knot growing in her throat.

STORIES OF HOPE FOR CHRISTIAN WOMEN

He shared a dream about floating with Emily and many strangers up to the sky past the clouds. He said they floated very gently but quickly upward until they were standing in front of a grand, majestic gate. After the gates opened by themselves, a man with a long robe, a golden belt, and collar decorated with different stones came to greet them. Ben said he knew that man was Jesus and that he especially liked the big lion walking by Jesus' side. Then Jesus invited them to look around. Ben even laughed, as he shared that Emily would love to hear that there were no stoves in heaven. He also said he was surprised that the water had the most delicious flavor, because it was completely clear. He described the colors as very vibrant and said he felt happy in that place. He also mentioned that Jesus' face was glowing like the color of shiny bronze.

By the time Ben finished telling his dream, Emily could no longer hold back her emotions. As tears began to roll down her cheeks, she asked why he thought he had that dream. Ben smiled and then said it was so others would know Jesus was real and would want to go to heaven. Then Ben simply went to play, as he usually did in the mornings.

Emily began to cry for joy, thanking God for His help in reaffirming her faith. Of course, she also shared the dream with Benjamin, but he was still not ready to receive the blessing. It would be many years before Benjamin would have his own encounter with Jesus.

Hope in Action

God is the source of all help.

Write about a time when you cried out to God for His help and you are certain He responded. Then thank Him for it.

_____

_____

_____

_____

_____

Write about a situation(s) where you need to cry out for help to God. Then pray about it.

_____

_____

_____

_____

_____

Hope:
Isabel Held on to God's Promises

May the God of hope fill you with all joy and peace as you trust in him, so that you may overflow with hope by the power of the Holy Spirit.

Romans 15:13

*I*sabel, or Isa as her family called her, was too young to remember when her father disappeared from her life. Although she had seen him a few times growing up, she didn't feel connected or look up to him, as he would lie to her every time she saw him. He would promise to visit her often, but many years would go by before she would hear from him again. He would say he would take her out to a fun place one day, provide financial support, she would inherit his home, and many, many more things that he never did.

One of Isa's saddest memories of her father was around the time she was about eight years old. As she was walking with her mother to the bus stop, her mom stopped to talk to a man who seemed to be an old friend. Isa was not very interested in their conversation, so she simply stood next to her mom, daydreaming, as she usually did when she was bored. Then, her mama surprised her by asking if she knew who that man was. From her mother's tone of voice, Isa gathered that she was to know the gentleman, but she was truly clueless. She did not want to embarrass her mother and took a wild guess.

She softly asked, "Is it my second grade teacher?"

From their expressions, it was obvious she had guessed wrong. Her mother then quickly interrupted the awkward silence by stating that he was her father. Isa was shocked to hear that she was related to such a stranger. It was specially confusing, as she could not see any resemblance with such a tall and hairy man. But as usual, her father didn't say much to Isa and quickly disappeared, just as he had appeared, but not before promising he would see her soon. Needless to say, that did not happen.

As if Isa was not confused enough about who was her father, her mother had introduced her to several parental figures at different times. All the men had been nice, but they would vanish out of Isa's life when the relationship ended with her mom. Other male figures had been older cousins or uncles. Among all her male relatives, there was one Isa loved. Her Uncle Joe was only thirteen years older than her, but he was funny, loving, and a wonderful cook. And Isa sure loved to eat! Her uncle had lived with Isa and her family at different times, as he had never married. Interestingly, he had also never brought any special someone around the family. Isa did not think it was odd, but the adults sure seemed to think so, as they would often comment about it.

It was not until Isa became a young adult that she understood her uncle identified as a gay male, which of course did not matter to Isa, but sure seemed to impact her uncle. Uncle Joe appeared to experience feelings of shame and guilt for his sexual identity and long history of trauma. He seemed to cope with life by drinking heavily and using drugs. As much as Isa felt for her uncle's emotional pain and substance abuse, all she could think of doing was to pray for him, not judge him, encourage him, and remind him how loved he was by her and many in their family. With that said, she poured all the love she had reserved for a father into her uncle Joe. While her uncle struggled to show affection, she knew he loved her dearly.

Not until he became very ill and almost died did he become more open about his love for Isa and several other family members. Isa was so grateful her uncle had recovered from the severe illness, although everything took a turn for the worst. Uncle Joe announced one day to the family that he was leaving the U.S., as he wanted to be buried where he was born and in the same tomb as his mother. It was a terrible emotional hit for Isa and many others who begged, pressured, and tried to convince Uncle Joe not to leave, but his mind was made up. He was determined to move back to his country of origin.

As much as Isa and her family did not want to let Uncle Joe go, they were happy that at least he had recovered from his health problems. But there were still some concerns, as he had been told by his doctor he could die if he drank again.

Within months of Uncle Joe's move, Isa heard that he had started drinking, which everyone feared could kill him. He was an adult, and it was clear that no one could force him to stop doing anything if he did not want to. Although several people had encouraged him to take care of himself, he didn't listen. It was no surprise, then, when Isa received a call from her sister informing her that their uncle was seriously sick and the doctor was giving a very poor prognosis. Isa became very saddened with the news, but more than anything, she was genuinely concerned for his soul. She began praying more than ever for him, hoping for a miracle, so that he could accept Christ in his life.

Within days of hearing that her uncle's health had worsened, Isa and some other family members took the first flight out of the country to visit him. When the family finally arrived at the hospital, she was devastated to learn from the medical staff that her uncle could no longer respond to external stimuli. He simply lay in a white room, covered up to his chest with a thin sheet. The doctors seemed to have given up on him, but Isa would not lose hope. She even told the main nurse she believed he knew they were there, but she just looked at Isa with sympathy, as the doctor has stated her uncle's mind was completely unresponsive. Isa did not lose faith in God and after praying, she began to talk to her uncle. To everyone's surprise, he gently squeezed her hand. Isa and her sister began to pray more over him and led him to Christ.

Although he could not move or talk, he accepted Christ by squeezing Isa and her sister's hands. Isa also reminded him that all his sins, no matter how big, had been forgiven in that moment, as he had accepted Jesus as his Savior. That was when her uncle squeezed her hand a little harder. Then Isa began to pray with tears in her eyes for God to call him home instead of giving him back his health, if he was not going to later follow Christ. Soon after that, her uncle stopped complaining of pain and passed away in an incredible, deep peace. It was by far the hardest prayer Isa ever had to do. It was also one of the saddest and happiest day of Isa's life.

Hope in Action

May the hope in Christ give strength to those who suffer physical, emotional, or spiritual anguish.

Write about a time when you did not lose hope, believing God could carry you through a difficult situation. Then thank Him for it.

_____

_____

_____

_____

_____

Write about a situation(s) where you need more hope. Then pray to God about it.

_____

_____

_____

_____

_____

Identity:
Martha Found Her True Identity

~

But our citizenship is in heaven. And we eagerly await a Savior from there, the Lord Jesus Christ.

Philippians 3:20

Martha's family immigrated to the United States from Mexico when she was in elementary school. The move was very challenging for her. She missed her friends, school, home, food, language, and everything else that she felt she was being forced to change overnight. She suddenly was expected to leave behind the only way of life she knew, to assimilate into a new culture. And while some of the aspects of the move were positive for her family, as a child, she did not always appreciate or understand it. For Martha, surviving in school and in her new neighborhood was her primary focus.

Unfortunately, she quickly found herself feeling like an outsider. Additionally, succeeding academically and socially was very difficult, due to her inability to speak English. There was also the discrimination she encountered in school with some of the other children and even some teachers.

The challenges she was facing in the new country saddened and discouraged her so much. She reached a point her stomach would hurt just thinking that she would have to go to school. In particular, being required by her teacher to read in front of the class and work out a math problem on a daily basis was the worst thing, as the other children would openly laugh at her heavy accent. It was especially hard for her, as she had been a great student in her native country, but felt was being treated as incapable or lazy, which she was neither. On the contrary, she was a hard worker, but it took time before she could speak the new language.

When Martha was finally feeling more comfortable in her new environment, her mother unexpectantly announced that they would be moving back to Mexico. Moreover, the family would be crossing the USA and Mexican border on a daily basis for Martha and her siblings to attend school, while her mother would go to work. To say the least, she was shocked to hear the news, as she finally had friends she could communicate with and was doing so much better in school. While she didn't like the idea of having to move again, she was happy about not having to endure discrimination any longer. But she never expected that moving back to her own country would be more challenging than when she first left.

To Martha's great surprise, the Mexican children treated her different for not going to school with them and not celebrating the same holidays. On the other hand, her school classmates in the United States were still treating her as an outsider. She was so confused, she didn't feel truly connected to either culture, but had to endure feeling rejected on both sides of the border.

As Martha became an adult, she remained unclear about which culture she belonged to. In a sense, her upbringing had tremendously impacted her personal identity. But all that changed after she became a believer in Christ. In her new faith, she not only healed from all the bullying and other types of trauma she experienced growing up, but she also found her true identity. The more she read the Bible and became part of the Christian faith, the more she discovered she had a place where she truly belonged. A place where she felt loved, welcomed and accepted in many places around the world. She also learned that regardless of where she came from, what language she spoke, or anything else, she was made in the image of the Father, saved by the Son, and was given the Holy Spirit to guide and comfort her. She finally knew who she was and what her final address would be!

Hope in Action

May all of God's children, find their true identity in Christ.

Write about the role God plays in your personal identity. Then thank Him for it.

_____

_____

_____

_____

_____

Write about a situation(s) where you feel like an outsider or alone. Then pray to God about it.

_____

_____

_____

_____

_____

Obedience:
Veronica Obeyed the Voice of God

~

Blessed rather are those that hear the word of
God and obey it.

Luke 11:28

*N*ever in a million years would Veronica have imagined that
would happen to her. Was she dreaming? Was she imag-
ining? Was she simply hearing what she wanted to hear, as
some later said? Veronica was not sure, but she sat there in
disbelief, hearing a powerful, yet kind and loving voice directed
at her. She was not praying for a miracle. Veronica was only
asking for God's guidance, as she found herself at a crossroads
and needed His direction.

What she heard that morning amazed and confused her all
at the same time. God was actually responding in an audible

voice and she knew it was Him. Most believers hope to hear God, but do not really think that will take place. Yet it was happening to her, and instead of focusing on the occurrence, she was disappointed by what she was hearing: "Be a Christian counselor."

That was not the answer she was looking for. She was asking God whether to open up a small pastry shop or participate in a self-paced online college business program to run her bakery in the future. She first wondered: Where did His response come from? Did God not understand her question? His answer made no sense to her, as she came from a culture where the word *counselor* or *psychologist* was not common. It was all too confusing, so she thought she could just ignore it. As if that was possible!

As expected, that was not the case, and she continued to hear the same phrase for days. Eventually, she also began hearing, "My people perish for lack of knowledge." That second comment really confused her. What in the world was a modest stay-at-home wife supposed to do about that?

As time went by, Veronica concluded she needed to share her experience with someone. She wanted to hear what another Christian would say and wondered if he or she would think she had lost her mind. After gathering enough courage, and with fear in her voice, she told her husband about what she had been hearing for days. To her astonishment, he did not seem surprised. Instead, he asked two simple questions that shocked Veronica to her core: "Are you sure it is God, and if so, are you going to obey?"

She could not believe her spouse actually thought she should give up on her dreams of being a baker. And then, how could she possibly respond to his second question in a way that would justify disobedience to the Creator? Out of words, she simply walked away. Needless to say, it took longer before she dared to pray about that same matter, only this time, she was ready for God. She told Him about her confusion with His answer, but eventually agreed to visit the closest University to her home and find out what it would take to do what He was asking from her.

Not long after that, she returned home with a binder and a class schedule. Veronica could not understand how God thought that she could possibly attend college and take care of her three children whom she homeschooled, along with all the other responsibilities of a stay-at-home mom.

Veronica spent the next years almost literally as a child throwing a tantrum. Although she was doing wonderful in her school program and was able to keep up with her home responsibilities, she complained over and over about being in a field she had not chosen. Then one day, as she sat in her office providing counseling services to a homeless, hungry and lonely patient, she realized why God had called her to serve. God wanted to use her feet, hands, mouth, and everything else to help His people heal and remind them of His great love. There it was! The answer she had been looking for. She had it all wrong; it had never been about her. Instead, she was reminded of her real purpose in the world.

Humans were created for God, not the other way around. And even then, He had not forced Veronica to obey Him, she had exercised her free will to listen to His voice because of her love for Him. From personal experience, she knew very well that there is great blessing in obedience to Him. From that day forward, she began to do her counseling job as if she was doing it for her Creator. In the process, her faith was strengthened and ultimately many people's lives were blessed because of her obedience to God.

Hope in Action

Is there something God is calling you to do? If so, are you going to obey?

Write about a time when you were blessed because you obeyed God's word. Then thank Him for it.

_____

_____

_____

_____

_____

Write about a situation(s) where you need to obey God's word. Then pray to Him about it.

_____

_____

_____

_____

_____

Peace:
Gloria Experienced Peace in the Midst of a Crisis

⌒

And the peace of God, which transcends all understanding, will guard your hearts and your minds in Christ Jesus.

Philippians 4:7

Gloria and her husband, Thomas, were very hardworking people. They both had made great sacrifices to attend college. As a result, they had obtained jobs that allowed them to pay their bills comfortably and to treat themselves to a few pleasures. You could say they had reached a somewhat financially stable place in their lives, which allowed them to begin to put into action many of their dreams. They had planned to build a casita in their property for Gloria's parents and a swimming pool for Thomas. They were both so happy with the direction their finances were taking and grateful for the possibility of accomplishing all their future plans.

In particular, Gloria was in constant gratitude to God for all His undeserved goodness and wanted to honor Him with every aspect of her life. With that said, she often wondered if her husband's unique spiritual beliefs could negatively impact the family. She wished more than anything that he would align his beliefs with the Bible, but he had his own ideas.

Thomas was a kind man with sincere intentions to know God better. However, in his continuous personal search for what he called the "the truth," he had become unclear about who God, Jesus, and the Holy Spirit really were and the purpose for creation. He would spend much time researching various belief systems, to the point he had started to think that everyone, no matter their spiritual views or their choices in this world, would all end up in the same blessed position with the Creator.

On the other hand, to Gloria, a strong believer in the Bible and everything in it, her husband appeared to be moving away from God's knowledge. Uncommon for them, they had even begun to have arguments when he would share his research with her or when she would tell him about her spiritual concerns for the family. A few times, during moments of great frustration, Gloria had even reminded her husband that per the Bible, he would answer to God about the family's spirituality. There had also been other times when she had made him feel responsible for their son's questioning of God's existence, insisting that his lack of Christian leadership was, in part, to blame.

For years, Gloria had fasted, prayed, and asked other believers for help, but she was feeling out of ideas and strength. Then, one day during one of her daily moments with God, she poured out her heart to Him and shared that she felt inadequate as a wife to support her husband and continue to encourage him spiritually. She then begged for help and asked Him to take control of the situation, as she did not have energy to help her spouse. From that moment forward, she felt more at peace, knowing she had given the situation to God. To encourage herself, she would quote Bible verses in her prayers: "And if we know that he hears us, whatever we ask, we know that we have what we asked of him" (1 John 5:15) and "Being confident of this, that he who began a good work in you will carry it on to completion until the day of Christ Jesus" (Phil. 1:6).

For a short period, it seemed to Gloria as if God had not answered her last prayer. That is, until the morning she picked up Thomas' cell phone. As she and Thomas were driving to the store to buy some last-minute items for a birthday party, his coworker called. Since Thomas was driving, Gloria put the phone on speaker, to find out that his whole department at work had been closed and Thomas was out of a job. Gloria was in shock and could not believe Thomas had been let go that same day. Nothing but a tap on the shoulder, a last paycheck, and a small box with some of his belongings had been given to him, as he was rushed out of his employer's building.

Thomas told her he had not wanted to ruin their son's birthday celebration, so he had planned on telling everyone the next day, but his coworker had gotten ahead of him. If possible, Gloria asked her husband to keep to his original plan and not discuss the situation any further until the following day, after church.

It was much easier said than done, because all Gloria could think of was her husband being let go. Her mind would jump from one scenario to another, as Thomas was the primary breadwinner and they had no more savings, due to having paid some large debts in preparation for future plans. She wondered how long it would take for him to find other employment or whether they would need to sell their home. She than began to think of her dreams for her parents. What about her sons' college and all the other plans they had? As hard as it was, she waited as agreed to the next day, which was Sunday.

During church and with discrete tears in her eyes, she prayed for God to give her the assurance that He was in control of the unexpected situation her family was facing. Then in the middle of a worship song, the Holy Spirit guided her to give her husband a message from Him. She was to tell Thomas that it was God working on him. As challenging as she thought it would be for her husband to hear, she knew she had to do it.

As she was contemplating how she would tell her husband, Gloria suddenly felt a deep peace take over her mind and body. She almost felt happy about their situation. Her calmness and overall joy did not match the circumstances. She just knew God was in control and everything would work out for the best. But Thomas was not as encouraged as her when she gave him the Holy Spirit's message. He simply responded with a gentle nod, but nothing else. Gloria did not know what to think of his response, but that was only the beginning of what was to come.

As weeks, then months passed, her husband became discouraged and depressed due to not finding employment as quickly as he had hoped. Even after many employment applications and job interviews, he would hear "no." But the bills kept piling up and he became anxious and frustrated multiple times. There was even a day he shared with Gloria his disappointment at not being able to provide for his family. He just could not believe that even with all his work experience he was unable to find a job. But Gloria was sure in her heart God would take care of them, which He certainly did. Even when the numbers made no sense, there was enough for food, mortgage, utilities, and for all the needs of their family.

Then one day, Gloria came home from work to a letter her husband had written to God. In that letter, her husband was promising God that for one year he would stay away from all research outside the Bible and he would devote all the time he used for research into God's holy book. Her husband had even dated it and signed it. He wanted Gloria to be witness to his contract with God. Needless to say, Gloria was overjoyed. She could hardly contain her excitement and gratitude to God.

Interestingly enough, Thomas attended yet another job interview, which ultimately led him to great employment.

Hope in Action

Even when things make no sense, God can give His peace to go through turbulent waters.

Write about a time when you felt at peace because you knew God was in control. Then thank Him for it.

_____

_____

_____

_____

_____

Write about a situation(s) where you need God's peace. Then pray to Him about it.

_____

_____

_____

_____

_____

Pray
Virginia Prayed for a Friend

~

Therefore, I tell you, whatever you ask for in prayer, believe that you have received it, and it will be yours.

Mark 11:24

Virginia's husband, Julian, had been offered a great job, but it would require the family to move to another city. While she was happy for his work opportunity, she also knew it would mean many changes for her husband and their children, but specially for her. She was very close to one of her sisters and even more to her mother. It was a time before cell phones, but they would talk on the phone almost every day, about anything from what each would cook for dinner to sharing their life struggles and successes. They would also see each other often for family events or just because they wanted to spend time together.

Additionally, in her culture, Virginia was expected to play a more active role in helping to care for her mother. From medical appointments to helping her run errands, making calls, lending an ear when she needed encouragement, or just to vent, she was there for her as much as possible. Then there was also Virginia's best friend Ana. Virginia and Ana had been friends since their teens. They had grown up together, which meant sharing many tears and laughs.

There were just so many reasons why Virginia didn't want to move. However, she knew above all other things, she needed to go where her husband went. She also believed the new job was a blessing from God, so how could she complain too much about the move? Nevertheless, she could not help feeling sad about what moving meant for her and the rest of the family. She was especially upset because she didn't want her children to miss growing up with their cousins or seeing their grandmothers as often. But sadness and all, the family packed up their belongings and went on their way to the new city. It would not be long before Virginia began to miss her old life.

The new city was literally a new city. Meaning it was still growing. There were no large supermarkets and the roads were almost empty. There were even people riding their horses on the streets, which she was not used to seeing. Then there was the struggle of trying to find a new church. Looking for a place to worship was really a challenge for the family, which meant going from one to another until they could find one that was similar to what they were used to. They also had to move within the new city a few times for work and finance-related issues, which made the changes even more difficult.

Virginia's husband and her children quickly adapted to changes. It was Virginia who missed her family, friends and her church the most. Being an introvert sure did not make it easier for her. Then came a ray of hope.

Virginia's family found a church they all liked. Her husband quickly began talking to other men and her kids made some friends through the children's ministry. But Virginia didn't have the same experience. While she became involved with some women's groups, she had a hard time finding a woman she could connect with. In part, it was her introvert personality and her anxiety about meeting new people. She grew really lonely and in need of someone she could trust and pray with, but it seemed to her that most ladies already had their close friends. Then it occurred to her: if she prayed about so many other things, why not pray for a friend?

That was exactly what she began to do. She prayed with faith for someone around her age, who attended her church, and with whom she could grow spiritually. As time passed, she would often remind herself that God hears His people's prayers and it would be in His perfect time. But even when it was taking longer than desired, she was hopeful that the answer to her friend prayer was around the corner. And of course, God always answers His children in one way or another.

Over time, Virginia met Mary, a woman who was just the way she prayed for. Mary was a married woman with children, who wanted to serve God and to grow spiritually, just like Virginia. Not long after meeting, the two began to share their life battles but also their spiritual wins. Since those days, they have remained best friends. As for the move, there have also been times when Virginia missed the way her new city used to be, as it had grown so much that they even had many large supermarkets, but also much more traffic everywhere she went.

Hope in Action

God will give to His children according to their faith and His plan for them.

Write about a time when you prayed with faith and received the answer to your prayer. Then thank God for it.

_____

_____

_____

_____

_____

Write about a situation(s) which requires you to pray and to wait on God.

_____

_____

_____

_____

_____

Strength:
Olivia Received Strength

God is our refuge and strength, an ever-present help in trouble.

Psalms 46:1

*O*livia had been in a romantic relationship with the same guy since her early teen years. As a woman in her twenties, she would pray that her boyfriend would propose and they would then have their happily ever after. She would imagine herself walking down the aisle of a church full of flowers, wearing a beautiful white dress, and her fiancé waiting at the end with his heart overflowing with love for her. She had also told herself she would stay a virgin and wear her white dress proudly, as she had been told only a virgin could wear white. On the other hand, her boyfriend would often test the limits of how far he could go sexually with her. To his disappointment, she would stop him every time and remind him that if he really loved her, he would respect her wishes and wait until their wedding night. Nevertheless, he would find ways to get her alone and try to go farther than holding her hand, a gently hug, or a sweet kiss.

In particular, one day after they had gone on a typical date, he took Olivia to a lonely area. He told her wanted to spend some time alone with her in a private place. While she had a good idea of what he might try, she knew her personal limits and trusted he would not cross them. To her surprise, this time it was completely different, as it was not him that posed a threat but what they encountered there.

Shortly after they parked the car, an explosion broke the car's driver side window. Since the sun had set and there was poor lighting, it was difficult to see. Additionally, they were both confused, as there was loud screaming coming from around the car. Suddenly, a male opened the driver's door, and pointing at them with a knife, instructed Olivia and her boyfriend to exit the vehicle. Once out of the car, the second armed male guarded Olivia and her boyfriend, while the first inspected the car for valuables. At that point, Olivia realized her boyfriend was bleeding profusely from his forehead. Then, the first man forced her boyfriend under the car, while the second dragged Olivia away with the intention to rape her. She was in shock and everything was happening so quickly; she felt as if she was in a horrible nightmare from which she could not wake up.

Her instinct was to pray and ask God for strength for them both to survive the situation. As one of the men began to touch her body, she was filled with great emotional strength and began talking to him in a calm voice. She first asked if he had any sisters or a living mother. Then she told him she wanted to serve God. To everyone's surprise, that man told the other not to abuse her, as she was a virgin. And while the second man didn't force her to have sexual intercourse, he did fondle her. Then, after stealing all the valuables, they threatened to kill Olivia and her boyfriend if they told anyone about them.

After the two men left, Olivia used a piece of her boyfriend's shirt to tie it around his forehead to stop the bleeding. Both were still so shaken up, and not knowing exactly what to do, they drove to her home. Olivia told her mother they had been robbed, but left out the details, for fear of her mother's reaction, and feeling shame for what she had just endured. Her boyfriend ended up needing stitches, but after having them removed and with a scar as a memory, he was much better.

Olivia was so grateful they had made it out alive and she was still a virgin, as they had later heard that other couples had experienced a similar situation, but the females had not been so lucky. Olivia knew God had given her the strength to speak up during the experience, to endure the trauma, and ultimately, to keep her virginity, which she saw as a great victory.

Hope in Action

God is the source of strength; it is up to each believer to tap into it.

Write about a time when God gave you the strength to do something difficult. Then thank Him for it.

_____

_____

_____

_____

Write about a difficult situation(s) that requires great strength on your part. Then pray to God about it.

_____

_____

_____

_____

_____

Trust:
Ivette Believed God Could Restore Her Marriage

Trust in the LORD with all your heart and lean
not on your own understanding

Proverbs 3:5

*I*vette had been married to Robert for over fifteen years. You could describe their marriage as stable, where there was good communication and the sharing of a home, children, and financial responsibilities, with the ups and downs of a typical relationship. However, both wanted more out of the marriage. While Ivette desired more romance and attention, Robert complained of the lack of passion in the bedroom. Ivette would buy books and suggest they go see a Christian couple's therapist, but Robert was not interested. Nevertheless, they had what appeared to others to be a wonderful relationship. Friends and family would often comment that they had an admirable marriage, as they always treated each other lovingly and respectfully.

Robert worked as an architect and Ivette was a teacher. While neither had ended in the professional field they had hoped, they both seemed content with having a job that helped pay the bills. He had given up on his dream to be a car racer, as it required much time and money, and involved many risks for him and his family. On the other hand, Ivette had originally wanted to be a medical doctor, but due to having children and other commitments, she was just thankful to be in a field where she could make a difference in others' lives. More than anything, she was grateful for the beautiful godly family they had.

Both Ivette and Robert identified as people of faith and were said to live according to strong Christian values. However, Robert had stopped being involved in any church ministry and seemed to be going through a period of spiritual questioning. Additionally, he had started working late hours and complaining about having given up on his car racing career. On the contrary, Ivette felt stronger than ever in her faith and invested much time in praying, serving, and encouraging everyone around her to know Christ. In particular, Ivette had been praying more than ever for her husband, as she had noticed him distancing himself not only from the church, but also from her and their children, which really concerned her, as it was not like him. But

Ivette ultimately thought it was a phase and continued to go about with her normal life, which included a praying ministry.

One evening, Ivette met with a strong Christian female who was visiting from another country. Ivette asked the Christian visitor if she would pray with her for a person in need, but to her surprise, the visitor insisted that the Holy Spirit was asking her to pray for Ivette first. After praying for Ivette, she told her to start praying specifically for God to reveal the truth about her husband. *The truth? What truth?* thought Ivette, but she trusted in God, using that woman to send a message, and began praying exactly as instructed.

Three days later, Ivette found out her husband was having an affair with one of the females he worked with. To say the least, Ivette was devastated, as she had always trusted in her husband unconditionally because she believed him to be a godly man. She was brokenhearted for herself, but her pain was even greater thinking of how it could affect their children, if the marriage ended. Feeling destroyed emotionally, she immediately went to God and began to pray over the situation and even asked her husband if he would allow her to pray for him. He agreed to the prayer, but up to that moment he had been denying having an affair and was blaming his behavior on Ivette, saying she did not make him feel desirable in bed.

When Ivette began to pray for her husband, the Holy Spirit repetitively guided her to give him a message, but she refused. She thought it was unfair that while she was hurting so much, God wanted to show His love to her cheating husband. Her husband was confused, as all he could hear was Ivette talking

STORIES OF HOPE FOR CHRISTIAN WOMEN

to herself and saying out loud that she wouldn't do it. Then in her mind, Ivette heard the Holy Spirit tell her, "Trust me!" and she broke down in tears and gave her husband the message.

She said, "God wants you to know that He allowed you to sin just enough, just enough to rescue you, as He loves you so very much."

Ivette's prayer was interrupted by her husband crying. It was obvious God's message had touched his heart. He admitted to the affair, said he was sorry, and he was willing to do anything to restore his marriage and not break his family apart. Ivette then told her husband that while she had lost all trust in him, she would stand in her trust in God and give him a chance to prove his sincerity to work on their marriage.

She asked him to call the woman he was having the affair with and break up with her via the phone, while Ivette would listen quietly. Her husband did call, and Ivette kept her word and sat in silence as the affair partner cried and begged her husband not to leave her. Ivette's husband then told the other woman it was over and that his wife had given him one chance and he was going to take it.

As difficult as it was for Ivette, she trusted God. Years later, their marriage is stronger, her husband is closer to God, and Ivette has been able to use her experience to help others going through a similar situation.

Hope in Action

Could we trust God with anything that we may be facing?

Write about a time when a situation in your life was resolved because you trusted in God and not in yourself. Then thank Him for it.

_____

_____

_____

_____

_____

Write about a situation(s) where you need to trust God and not lean on your own understanding. Then pray to Him about it.

_____

_____

_____

_____

_____

CPSIA information can be obtained
at www.ICGtesting.com
Printed in the USA
LVHW081203220720
661203LV00019B/1087